Soul
Whispers

A Collection of Spiritual Poems

By

Ana Maria Macra

ISBN: 987-1-7379948-0-0 (paperback)

Library of Congress Control Number: 2021922277

Cover design by Danielle Jaycox

First printing edition 2021, Romana Publishing

Love and support are what made this book possible. I want to thank my husband for inspiring me to pursue my dreams, and my children for showing me the true meaning of life. They're the foundation that supports me and the loving arms that catch me. They're home, they're shelter, they are unconditional love.

Contents

Author's note

Soul Whispers is a collection of poems selected from hundreds I have written. A couple of years ago, I had this crazy idea, this knowing, that one day I will write a book. At the time, the inner knowledge hardly matched my words. My mind was confused hearing the words come out of my mouth, but my soul knew them to be true. The soul is the fuel. I allowed it to consume me and burn all the doubts, and then I rose.

This book is a symbol of the lost girl rediscovering herself, her power, her purpose. It's a mental and spiritual transformational journey.

Read. Reflect. Read again. The poems are written in a purposeful way, the beauty is not only in the rhyme when the rhyme is present, but in the meanings the reader might unveil.

Between Mental and Spiritual

I only know that I don't know,
I only catch a glimpse
Of worlds unseen to naked eye,
In moments of abyss.

I stand between two worlds, at best,
I see, but I don't know.
There's no one to confirm or quest,
These visions that I'm shown.

I feel my peaceful Angels
Surrounding me with love,
They keep me safe and harmless
Into the eye of storm.

A fog is all around me
Creating fear; and hope
That when it'll all be over,
Humanity's awake.

It is a bitter feeling,

There's no light in sight,

Just trust in the Almighty

That comes in dreams at night.

I'm here, my hearth is aching,

I understand so much,

But words are all too little,

And too many frozen hearts.

I'd share with all my knowledge,

But most don't want to hear,

Most don't believe in miracles,

And worlds beyond the veil.

All that I have's a voice,

Much stronger in my head

Than when I use their words

Too little to transcend.

There's a vast world inside me,
I feel it growing bigger
With every piece of knowledge
I see in rear-view mirror.

I'm never good with words,
It's hard to clearly express
The feelings that disturb
My fitting in this race.

I felt misunderstood and lonely,
Took cover in within,
I found a world that's magical
And peaceful to live in.

It's sweet in here, it's loving,
I dwell in here a lot,
I faintly hear some voices
Summoning me outside.

But these voices are mental,
They don't speak to my soul.
My soul is free inside me,
In my magical world.

They'd all fit there if they'd want to
Take shelter from despair,
Observe the world and then renew
Their principles and glare.

I feel, within, connected,
To the ones that we once were,
Pure souls in the beginning,
Released now in the world.

Once, all we had was kindness,
And knowledge from Divine,
Now I'm at peace, and I sense,
We'll go back there, in time.

And we shall conquer heavens,
We'll get what's rightfully ours,
We'll humbly bend our knees
With grateful hearts and flowers.

And then, we will be free,
Lack heaviness on hearts,
The fight, then, will be over,
And angels we'll become.

For others, it'll start again,
The cycle to enlightenment,
And we will watch for them
The paths of life in this land.

We'll help, but they won't see us,
Just like we don't see now
Our angels all around us,
Protecting anyhow.

There's love to be discovered,

It sleeps inside in all,

And it is growing stronger

Right here, inside our soul.

It'll lift us up to greatness,

It is the only way

To ends this journey-cycle,

And free us from the slay.

It is the only purpose,

During this life on earth,

To find and spread the kindness

And free the path to God.

Cycles

Worlds as we know
Are not meant to stay,
Caught in the cycle
Of time and non-time.

Being reborn
Wiser and stronger
When reaching the end,
And beginning of time.

One cycle is ending
Overlapping a new one,
Higher consciousness passing
In another dimension,
Leaving behind
The low and the dark.

Old souls are they
In the new world creating,
Teachers and wise
For the new souls born in.

Higher consciousness moving
To a brighter cycle,
More evolved and intense,
With no restriction of time and space.

Vishuddha Earth

When the Big God had blasted us in Universe

He placed our home, the Earth, in perfect spot,

So we can still feel the warmth, and hear the voice
of reason,

So we can still see the face of godly Sun.

He chose this spot so we can see Him clearer,

So we're not burnt and blinded by His light,

So we don't linger icy in a freezer,

Or make excuses that we were placed too far.

He placed us in His throat so we can hear His voice,

To feel the air like seasons, in the airway passing,

In words too sweet, and sometimes moist,

According to our actions and our lapsing.

We're lumps on throat on the Divine Creation,

Not knowing when to swallow or to spit

We're facing weather variation,

He's undecided on tornadoes, or the sink.

He's sending clear signs, though lava and through storms,

That we so blindly take as tea with lots of honey,

We hear the thunder loudly piercing in His throat,

Itched by the trees that fall exchanged for money.

We're thinning out His beneficial flora,

Dooming our planet to un reversible harm,

We eat through His beloved fauna

And wonder why we're tired and feel down.

We're anchored equally between the heart and mind

So we can reach through love illumination,

We were the most beloved of them all

And the most beautiful in God's creation.

Self-love

The way we love and value others
Is merely a reflection of self-love.
We hurt ourselves, then we hurt others,
We love ourselves, then we love others,
We heal ourselves; we love them more.

It is through eyes of love we shine the brightest,
It is through love we open doors
Toward the heart where worlds are widest,
Where love resides, lightning unbiased
Inside the center of the soul.

What is self-love you might inquire?
It is the power to stand tall,
To do what's right, through thorns and fire,
And more important,
The absence of thought poisoning the soul.

Freedom

It's time to search inward,
To look deep within the soul,
To purge the old beliefs
Passed on by centuries of hurt.

It's time to start anew,
Unclothe the pain and hate,
Keep what is pure in you,
Tear open your crate.

There's more to life than pain,
And you should feel the rising
Of soul when you unchain
The gates of hurt and suffering,

Release what has been done
To you, across the lifetimes.
Re-set your spirit free,
And fly toward the sunshine.

14

Live in the now

Leave all there is behind,
Step into the light,
Become light.

Let the light fill up your whole being,
Absorb the light energy,
Absorb the calm, the knowledge,
The unconditional love, and the objective.
The righteousness.
The now.

Now is all there is outside the time.
Time is creating a split in the now,
An illusion of timelines.

We live now, and now is eternal.
The notion of time does not exist in the eternal,
Time was created for, and by the physical mind.
Now is not physical yet exists.

Now is all, and all is now.

A consciousness seen, yet unseen

Living outside time and space,

Outside the laws of the physical.

Affirmations

I'm a lover of souls,
I don't like attachments,
The true and the bold
Are my heart's commandments.

I'm kind, I'm salty, I'm brave,
All in one,
I don't care for pity,
I'm determined, polite.

I'm surrounded by peace,
I have joy in my heart,
I carry my days
With clear thoughts in mind.

I'm honest and fierce,
I don't bend in the wind,
I've created my world
Without lies or prejudice.

I'm stronger each day,

Abundantly empowered,

Blessed, unafraid

To pay it forward.

I'm loving, supportive,

Caring, uplifting,

Patient, rewarding,

Humbly living.

I'm nurturing, gentle,

Faithful and warm,

Altruistic, responsible

Generous and calm.

Observe, don't absorb

In worlds of feelings inside me
A word or stare creates a bridge,
A path for soul to travel in,
And feel your thoughts as you were me.

I've struggled long time to control
The pull to visit every soul,
The pain I saw, it made me sick,
I felt it mine; it was mirroring.

I shut that door so I can heal,
Gave myself years recovering,
And in the day I felt most safe,
I opened the door to just observe.

I saw the choice and the free will
As servants, standing next to me.
Anchored my soul in principles,
Values to seek in individuals.

I peaked in souls then, just to test

Which one of all fits mine the best.

I found that all are quite unique,

But mine I seek, sits next to me.

Shadows

You're following me through time and space,
In lifetimes over lifetimes,
I was a child back then, and I was scared,
But now I grew, and now I'm not afraid.

A little girl, just playing in the palace,
I threat I was, because you knew I'll grow,
I'll find, and I will stand in power,
And in that moment, you'll rule no more.

You scared me, and you pushed me,
Behind the throne I hid.
My father, the land's rightful ruler,
He was protecting me.

But I got lost in panic,
My memories suppressed,
You hoped I won't remember,
And you'll have time to rest.

As newborn, in this world,

And as a little girl,

When asked what I'd become,

A queen! I said to all.

And now, that I grew stronger,

My memories come back.

I'll fight, and I will conquer,

And bring the right queen back.

You threw me in this world

And thought I would forget

Of who I really was,

And how to get right back.

The pain, you thought, will break me,

In fact, it made me stronger,

And in my rule, I will be

Much better and much wiser.

Vision

In a symbolic vision I just saw
The worlds clashing, crashing, and destruction,
Cause there's no place above for all
That didn't learn in time the earthly lesson.

The hateful, spiteful, crawling on this earth,
Blinded by power, attached to earthly goods,
Along with assets, they all will slowly burn
Before a new world will come to set its roots.

They will be cursed, like others before them,
To crawl beneath the rays of light.
They will still hate, despise the world to come
Because their face will only see the night.

They'll be forgotten, lurking in the dark
With weak attempts to feed on human soul,
And though they'll see them, humans are too high,
And their hunger can satiate no more.

23

Imagine heaven

I've been to heaven in my dream,
It was so...heavenly.
They showed me things, and how it works,
It made all sense to me.

It is quite simple honestly,
It is all but love and light,
And everything is done fully
From goodness of the heart.

I loved it there, I might go back
If they allow me to,
But until then, I'll stay on track
And do just what I do.

I'll sit here quietly, and whisper,
To those that want to hear,
Our world is spinning quietly
But our angel's always near.

I woke up with a joy in heart

And confidence that we're

Just moving to a start

Much better, and much clear.

It gave me strength to spread the word,

To those ready to hear,

That this is really not the end

On our rocky sphere.

Is it really that bad?

Is it really that bad
We're forced to slow down?
Is it really that bad
We slowed the speed of time?

The world felt confused
On the run every day,
We needed a break
To reflect and to pray.

We had to catch up
With what's profoundly important,
We sacrificed hearts
To fit in a carton.

We checked many boxes
Of earthly desires,
We fabricated phony causes,
And became just survivors.

Our purpose is different,

We come to find out,

It entitles commitment

For love, and soul growth.

We created the tools

To help free up time

For what's meaningful,

For a happy life.

It became now addiction,

We create more and more,

It is all competition

And rarely teamwork.

But tables have turned,

Now we're forced to stay put

And look in the eyes

Of the ones that we hurt.

We ask for forgiveness
From the souls that we hurt
So we can enjoy meals
And savor desert.

At the table together
Time seems to stay still
As we pray to our Father
To allow us to live.

Live and let live

Live and let live makes every day more sense,

We're trained to recognize power as status and
wealth,

We look up to the rich while we enter a cage

With walls so thin, we hear their voices of death.

We hate MLM but we enter it daily

Allowing others to dictate our worth,

Not seeing we're mistaken gravely

Thinking of freedom while we move back and forth.

We're vessels for souls, and the soul is power,

Waiting to be awakened and reach for the sky,

To connect once again with the source, like a tower,

Invisible connection to the earthy eye.

We're specks of divine, able to grow

Powerful, strong, protected by right,

Bits of universe with unrevealed glow,

While they, just darkness disguised in light.

29

Just pray

Pray for your neighbor,
Pray for your wrongdoer,
Don't sip from their hatred,
Don't poison your soul.

Plant the seed of kindness
You wish to see tomorrow,
Pave the way for cycles
Returning to this world.

You see it's a hard battle,
We fight with the dark forces,
Don't send them out as cattle!
You'll hear their pain in voices.

You'll be unseen to them
But you will hear them still,
You'll feel as yours the pain
Of worlds that you could heal.

Don't sell your soul for battle

For freedom's gained through war,

Keep energy for later

When the worlds will clash and roar.

Split

Are we forsaken?

Are we forgotten?

Did the consciousness pass,

Or it's in full process?

Are we still crawling?

Are we yet walking?

Did the division happen,

Or we're still together?

Are the souls captured?

Are they awakened?

Are they here blending,

Last lessons learning?

Are the eyes blind?

Did they become kind?

Are they simply observing,

Or critically inspecting?

Are we still human?

Are we illusion?

Are we still clothed in flesh,

Or just drowning in stress?

Is the kindness long gone?

Is it pests we've become?

Is love overrated,

Or by possessions weighted?

Is it still day and night?

Did our vision adapt?

Is it light disguised dark,

Or we're feeding from though?

Are we still the beloved?

Are our days numbered?

Is it the end of our time,

Or the ascending up high?

Path

I thought I lost my flow,

I took a detour,

Admired other aspects of life,

I saw I could fit in,

But my thirst wasn't quenched.

That path can be intense and addictive,

A tangled distraction in reality of time,

With many followers, and eyes that see

Corners of matrix when the mirrors turn.

Drove back to a path of deep understanding

Where time exists not.

It's but light creating a response in the soul,

A knowledge without words.

Unity in all

Freely I give support, and some knowledge
To the seeker of life with better outcome,
Bound by my heart with the promise I pledge
To myself, to the one I become.

I grow, and along with me I raise the ones willing
To evolve, and expand in directions unknown,
Implying that the skies are not worth seeing
Without confronting the demons we own.

We grow even more when we stand together,
When doing what's right with love and respect,
Or abandon the ascension alone, altogether,
Cause evolving alone will meet a reject.

There's purpose for being in human experience,
And growth is achieved in unity's lock
Cast by the universe in a place of resilience,
When the bond, and the love for creation was lost.

We've deepened our sin, we turned all self-centered,

We demand recognition for irrelevant acts

Praying in secret our sins won't be suspected

When lips are tied, and pain locked in heart.

Inner Strength

Did you feel the power inside
When you envisioned what you want in life?
Hold it, maintain it, feed it,
Draw your strength from it.

Was your soul burning with desire
To strive and raise your spirit higher?
That flame has power to burn through
The useless chatter stopping you.

You felt the doubtful voice completely fading
When you made plans towards life's mending?
It's just the start to a brighter path
Of peaceful, loving work of art.

You sometimes hear external voices
Looking to dim your hard-worked progress?
They're bugs attracted by your light
Wanting to shine on your spotlight.

You found yourself in eye of storm

With voice of doubt being your own?

Return to what has sparked your plan,

Retrieve that fuel and go on.

You feel the flame is growing bigger

Achievement fueling your joy inner?

Just know the path you choose fits right,

And life from now on will be bright.

Uncage Jesus

It will get worse before we're saved,
We say it on and on
Waiting for Jesus to return,
And free what we've enslaved.

The pride won't let us see we're wrong,
We are oppressing souls.
There's no color skin in eyes of God,
Just souls sent in this world.

There's never peace in parts of world,
Though Jesus is in all,
He is held captive by the mind
That rules earth and beyond.

I'm asking you to free Him,
Allow Him to come free,
And make Him proud of people
And souls that we can be.

The pride and the deceitful,

It doesn't serve us right,

For all the souls are equal

Seen through the eyes of God.

Free Him, and you shall free

The love and understanding,

The inner peace that we all need,

In the new world we're planning.

Rising of Soul

Surrender thy soul
To the wisdom of Light,
Take ye the knowledge
And follow thy path.

Of this world are ye,
But of this world ye are not,
Ye were born into Christmas
In times of the dark.

Take ye the wisdom,
And travel the stars
To burn ye the darkness,
And shine in the light.

Up in the Heavens,
Where thou shall be free,
Conquer great wisdom
For those born onto thee.

Show them the stars,

Show them the path,

Teach them great wisdom

To shine through the dark.

Pass them the knowledge

So they can be free.

Sons of the starlight,

Born from the light.

Surround them with wisdom

And messages-key,

For a path that will lead them

In the stars next to thee.

Open the pathway,

So they can go through,

To reach out the light

And come next to you.

Surrender

Surrender thy body,
And reach for the light,
For only the knowledge
Can take you high.

Accept ye thy fate,
Surrender thy body,
Your knowledge and wisdom
Will shine from within
Protecting and caring,
On ways through the starlight
Till the end of times.

Protecting and caring
From eyes of the night
That carefully watch ye,
And waiting to take ye
From the right chosen path.

Surrender and listen
To the words from above,
For they will guide ye
Through the magic of life.

Be brave and be humble,
And listen with care
To the words of the wisdom
Laid out on the way.

Thy path to the knowledge
Might look like a maze,
Meaning to keep ye
From the chosen, right way.

Listen the voices,
They guide ye the way
Leading to knowledge
Beyond the veil.

You're eager to listen
And shed some light
On the knowledge well hidden
Deep in the dark.

The knowledge is here
Waiting its seekers,
Waiting to give them
The wisdom of time.

When earth was just matter,
Before the bright light,
Waiting for people
To walk on its paths.

And out of the darkness
Arose a new life,
Guarding the children
Just born by the Light.

45

Gratitude

You took me far and sheltered
My being in this world,
You always heard my prayers,
And now I understand.

You gave me what I asked for
And more, just what I need,
To wake at dawn in new world
And see crumbles at me feet.

You show me now the reason
It was not fit for me,
It drowns with every season
In pits too deep to see.

I praise You once again,
I feel You more and more,
And now I understand
I have a role in all.

And though I'm feeling ready,
More confident each day,
You project lessons for me
To learn and to obey.

My heart is feeling grateful,
I feel my spirit expanding,
I see that being faithful
Has brought me understanding.

Awakening

Have you ever stopped and wondered
What awakening really is?
Close your eyes to world outside you,
Open them to worlds within.

Know yourself, divine and demon,
Dust the fears haunting you
Till you see that in the mirror
The white wolf is watching you.

Draw your strength from spirit's well,
Drink from spirit's wisdom fountain,
Feel pulsating every cell,
And your universe expanding

You will learn in time that distance,
Space, and time are merely measures,
Making sense to our world here,
Not applying to our universe.

There, the wings, and cars are useless,

Years, as we have here, too.

Spirit's free to travel chargeless

In the higher conscious's pool.

Live and let be

The messages keep coming through
In visions, dreams, and feelings too.
I'm shown so many to remember
Since began writing that September,

The trigger's simply words of God,
And looking deeply in the heart
With quiet mind, and labels free,
Just making space for the unseen.

It went from terrors scaring me
To angels guarding over me,
Whispering softly in my ear
Facts, when I was strong enough to hear.

They send me visions or big screens
With what's unfolding, so I see,
Sometimes repeating endlessly
Things to remember in 3D.

And just last night, in lucid dreams,

They showed events coming to be,

Drawing conclusions loud to hear

To live and let the others be.

Faith

I lay my life in your hands
With faith that I'll be safe,
And I will do a work
I've chosen to engage.

I've opened up my heart
For others to embrace,
To help, support, and love
My peers in this cold place.

So they can feel through me
A touch of godly angels,
In darkest days to see
Your love for your creation.

I entrust my heart to you,
You fill it up with kindness
So I can spread it through
This world with signs of jaundice.

They're pale, cause they forgot
When spiraling through time,
Their face should always be in light
And hearts should always prime.

It seems the best reminders
Are darkest times, when come,
And vow through tears of blindness
They won't forget next time.

You're kind through endless revelation
And show us right from wrong,
You point the path to our salvation
Forgiving on and on.

It suddenly got quiet

The chatter stopped and I'm intrigued,
Where did the voices go?
What urgency and what great need
Has gathered spirits all?

The winds of change are blowing soft,
A break is what we earned,
Return they with the news and chart,
New plans for peaceful earth.

We all had chances to get in,
The path from now but narrows,
The purest white for souls to seek,
That lights the path to new world.

From here on, there will be help
Only for souls in the transition,
The poison here, they will forget,
And have peace as retribution.

I'll be home

All I have are thoughts and words,

Too little words though

Trying to catch up with the train of thought,

And two slow hands attempting to paint the colors
of depth,

Two hands that linger in the onyx, hesitant to touch
the light at the end of the tunnel.

The eyes see and the mind reflects,

There's bliss in the travel, in the anticipation of end.

Staring at the light, delaying the fulfillment,
immersed in sublime

I draw the energy,

I sip life from the eternal yet remain on the road
inches away from the end, but far enough to see
both worlds,

Anchored in human but close enough to feel the
warmth of divine in a game I'll enjoy losing.

I'll be a speck in the golden, glowing in harmony
with the celestial,

I'll be in the home of playful giggles, of tranquility
and peaceful.

I'll be home.

I let go and I found love

I let go of the binding fear,

I let go of the need to be right,

Of being controlling,

and of the acceptance of being controlled.

I let go of being prideful, fitting, and seen.

I let go,

I plunged into the unknown that I once perceived
dark and scary,

In a free fall of choice

I touched the depths of fear,

The depths of solitude,

The depths of pain.

I cried and I hurt,

Felt empty and alone in that home,

But I was home.

My home of shattered dreams, of shattered plans,
and hope...and love...

And I cried...and cried...

Despised myself for the betrayal of my own heart,
of my own soul that I so casually buried in the
dungeon of darkness, ignorance and obliteration.

I exchanged it for acceptance, for a stolen breath of musty air,

The leftover air, the crumbs, the chocking pressure...

In all my darkness, the tiniest window remained,

A symbol of hope,

The point of return.

The dustiest window the sun can still shine its rays through.

The hope. The only hope.

The only speck of what I once was,

The only seed of what I could be,

My bridge,

My rainbow at the end of the storm.

I let go of everything and I found my Self in a seed,

The biggest joy in a particle of light,

And I bloomed...and I'm blooming...and I'm growing,

Filling my soul-cage with my Self,

With my love,

Ever expanding, ever bright, ever brighter

Till soul breaks free, and fear is gone.

I rebuilt myself with love, through love, in the name of love and freedom,

With patience, and grace.

I'm walking my path up the rainbow to light,

My tears have become a well of joy,

I stopped waiting to be seen, and I saw myself,

I stopped waiting to fell loved, and I loved myself,

I stopped waiting to be accepted, and I accepted myself,

I stopped waiting to be pieced, and I was whole,

I filled the gap of longing for myself with my Self.

I chose me so I can offer from the heart, and not to give borrowed, ill, and misfit layers of labels, opinions, and shoulds.

I chose me, through me, for all. The world is better with me than it is with projected layers around me.

I found peace,

I found acceptance,

I found freedom,

I let go and I found love.

We will vacation in the mountains

We will vacation in the mountains
During the summer's scorching heat,
Feeling the breeze and energies
Of fluttered wings surrounding in.

We will vacation in the mountains,
Discover selves and soul within,
We'll drink from wisdom's endless fountains,
We'll hear the music in the wind.

We will vacation in the mountains,
It'll bring us closer to the Earth,
It'll bring us closer to our founders,
We will hear whispers of our worth.

We will vacation in the mountains
Quenching the thirst of worlds we miss,
We'll understand they are no phantoms,
Just souls forgotten and dismissed.

We will vacation in the mountains

Filling our cup with joy and peace,

We'll raise our spirit up the highest,

And far from darkness's deep abyss.

Assisted Passing

I see through your eyes, so quiet and joyful,

I feel what you feel, free of the bonds of past life.

You returned to your home, your happy place always,

Your heart fills with joy, as the life's chain released you.

You dwell in the place where you once had freedom,

You sit on the porch overseeing the south,

You look at your garden and the trees that have fed you

When life was yours to live as you pleased.

Your heart is full now, enjoying in silence.

Such feast for your eyes to look at your garden

With berries, and fruits, and trees abundant in love.

You missed all this freedom, you hungered for home,

For peace and for quiet,

For the pleasure of being free from the bond.

You glance through the life you lived, skipping
pain,

You see just the love and peace that it brought you

When life and decisions were just yours to make.

You move your attention to the coop where your
hens and the chickens roamed free.

You notice it's clean, and the stream of water is still
flowing through,

Peacefully flowing from the spring up the hill.

You're still in awe by the spring overflowing

Quenching the thirst of your hens and your plants.

You see it as blessing, a sign, and a knowing

That that was the place you belonged and brought
joy.

You worked all your life to create a safe haven,

You hoped you'll get to enjoy it when the storms
will have past,

But you knew deep inside the future's unstable,

And you longed for your home before you left it behind.

You mourn the decisions your heart didn't pass,

You wish to dwell here in this form that you got,

But your angels have told you you're allowed just to visit

In flashes of life you hoped to have had.

A sadness compels you as you turn to the garden

On the North side of house, where cucumbers grew,

To the field you surrounded with basil and jasmine,

And spirits felt ever present with you.

You see in a flash your sheep, so meek, and so loyal

Looking at you with sparks of love in their eyes.

The sadness now fills you, and the regret for the choices

You didn't feel to make in your heart.

You gave up your safe haven for a promise you knew it won't hold,

You embraced the decline of life in the peaceful,

You pleased the voice of strength and unkind.

You regret now not living the life you set for,

And you show me in feelings and pieces of image

The lack of decisions is the caging of soul.

Your beauty in spirit is kindness to learn.

You're fading. At peace in the darkness of day

You continue your journey through stages of life.

This was for me. To see through your eyes,

to show me my dreams of a life just like yours can bring joy,

And a peace for the heart to enjoy.

I send you love and gratitude in ways the mind can't comprehend,

In tongues that souls can apprehend,

When meet outside the time and space.

In worlds where souls are roaming free, able to send impressions, feels,

Communicate in thought of heart, fly unrestricted in the dark,

Shinning gold lights in joyful dance,

Tasting but freedom, happiness.

You still have long way, I can read

In thoughts you open just for me,

(and you're worried, I can see,)

You'll go to face the scary ones,

And to explain your painful acts.

You're scared, remorseful, soul is small,

The fear of judgement fills you all.

Open you soul, I send in thought,

I promise you it's not that bad.

You're judged for love you gave in life,

The deepest, purest, from the heart.

You hide in light a shameful truth

That's valid just for life on earth,

Release that fear, and shine your soul,

Let light of gold fill spirit all.

65

The fear up here is not a fact,

Belonging only in past life,

Let go of it and see your light,

It's shinning brighter in the night.

Your soul was good, mistakes you made

In earthly eyes of rules premade,

But here we count the blessings, love,

The change you brought for life on earth.

You see, regret is almost gone,

No need to hold memories long,

They'll pull you back in circles high,

And you'll relive them in the sky.

Release the prison of the past

Holding you back from stepping past

From this realm you see as grey,

With spirit's light paving the way.

The next realm you see as white,

Like fog and clouds up in the sky,

You see through it glimpses of green

And rays of sunshine filling in.

You see the vastest sea of green

Unfolding as you step within.

You feel the freedom in this space,

A place familiar, happy place.

You see them coming down the hill,

The ones you loved, welcoming you

With touch so warm, and kind, and soft,

Happy to see you coming back.

You feel unworthy, shameful, lost,

Your memories of them seem lost,

Your soul is ticking though, with joy,

Pulsing the love for them in joints.

You're still confused, looking at them,
You know no faces, only souls,
The souls familiar, souls you missed,
Under amnesia while you lived.

Your heart is racing, can't control
The happiness and joy of soul.
You stopped in place, feel paralyzed
As they approach you, smiling bright.

You stand, unable to advance
Until their welcome in this house,
And soul within can recognize
Soul family waiting above.

In thought, I read you're missing one,
And feel my worldly pain inside.
She is still here, the last of you,
Delay the call, I beg of you!

You say her pain out here will end,

And while my soul can comprehend,

My earthly heart still feels the pain…

At least I know I must prepare.

I see you held the fort for us,

While her soul roamed, paying a price.

You let her live, though empty house,

Her soul was brave, guarding above.

What lonely life she must have had

Keeping souls safe inside that land,

Battling demons at the gates,

Keeping souls out of the harm's reach.

And though it's hard, I must let go.

Her wish to make the circle whole

I sense so urgent, so complete,

I wish her peace and pray for it.

She feels she failed me all these years,
She asks approval to come near,
She pours the gift of love in heart,
My earthly skin now has goosebumps.

I now forgive her, set her free
To take her place with family.
With eyes of love, she looks at me,
Blessing my path, and blessing me.

She gives me gifts that fill the heart,
And confidence, and better sight,
She wipes my tears, she heals my heart,
She's planting seeds of love and art.

I wish to be as brave as her,
But she assures me that through her
My path in life will be complete,
With angels guarding over me.

She says my purpose is to see,
To learn, to feel, and grow within,
Between two worlds to be a bridge,
Shining the light for souls to see.

She missed me, and I feel her pain
And the regret I was alone.
She trusted me, she knew I can,
Had faith in me, and I returned.

She'll have to leave and take her place
Inside her circle of the souls.
She takes her place, filling the gap,
The ring of souls is unified.

She gave me voice, she gave me love,
She made me strong and confident,
And now I vow to honor her,
Stand for what's right, raise next to her.

I am the bridge, I touch their ship,
I light their path and so they leave
To higher realms, a brighter world,
Another place to grow and learn.

I see they are a bit unsure
Of what to expect in this new world,
I raise to them and sound it clear,
They're learning best without the fear.

I smile and know they'll do just fine,
I trust their leader, she was mine.
I bow in sign of great respect,
They will do great, I'm confident.

It's time for me to come back down,
Return the spirit and the light,
Until the light they'll need again,
And open path for them to ascend.

I feel content, with joy in heart,

I know that this is just the start

Of my own work among the stars,

By lifting souls to higher realms.

I'm grateful too, and humble most,

To have been chosen for this post,

To witness joy of life accomplished,

To light the path for those ascending.

I feel the freedom, happiness

My earthly body witnesses,

The wait is over, time to shine,

And leave the chains of past behind.

The love and kindness fill within,

The confidence keeps pouring in,

With my back straight, and vision high,

I pave the road towards the sky.

Whole

My arms stretched out,

My hands hold the future,

It's present.

As my arms bend, they clothe me,

And they fill me in dreams accomplished.

In my universe, I am where I was born to be,

I own me,

I am not the body,

I am not the soul,

I am not the journey,

I am the sum of everything.

I am not added,

I am not subtracted,

I am whole, and part of the whole,

I am.